The Adventure Crew

Dramalina the Elf

Dramalina is a proud and noble elf-maiden. She is the leader of the Adventure Crew and can be quite bossy. She LOVES adventure but doesn't like pickles.

Fakebeard the Great

Fakebeard is a shrewd and powerful wizard, known throughout the land as a great magician. And definitely not a lady.

Brian the Barbarian

Brian, son of Gondorr, is the strongest man in the land. He actually prefers reading to wrestling, and dreams of becoming a librarian barbarian one day.

Grimblegroo the Dwarf

Grimblegroo isn't really partial to adventure but he does like treasure, so he goes along with the others in case they find any.

Yes, she was pretty mad after that!

She was furious — hopping mud, you could say!

It's not funny, guys. The treasure chest is almost empty. Soon there won't be any money for biscuits.

Sigh. Maybe we aren't cut out to be adventurers ...

I mean, Brian, you like browsing books more than bashing goblins.

It says here that most bands of adventurers split up after two years.

Hocus-pocus, vac-there, vac-here — dirt and crumbs now ... DISAPPEAR!

Fakebeard, there is something weird about your wizardry.

9

Sigh! We'll never get past those ogres.

They're gigantic!

We will! We just need to think of a cunning and ingenious plan.

Hmm. Come on, Brian! Think ... Think ... Think ... Think ... Think ...

Finally, Brian comes up with a plan ...

I've got it! First, we need to build a large trebuchet, which is a catapult that will send us zooming over the supermarket walls. Then, Grimblegroo can distract the ogres by ...

Huh? Where did everyone go?

Brian! Over here!

Who said that?

It's me! Put on your cloak of invisibility!

17

Grimblegroo wanders off in search of a snack.

Mmmm. Yummy biscuits!

But these were no ordinary biscuits. These were enchanted monster biscuits!

Choc chip! My favourite!

Uh-oh!

Prepare to face my fury!

Where's Grimblegroo?

We're almost there. We just need to get through the freezer section.

SPECIAL OFFER!

Look out for polar bears and penguins!

Finally, our heroes arrive at the milk cabinet.

Yay! We did it! Now let's get Mum's milk and get out of here!

Look — I found a trolley.

So! You think you have defeated the Goblin King? Did you honestly think I'd let you buy milk that easily? Guards! Seize them!

Goblins!

Quick! Into the trolley!

Hurry Brian! They're gaining on us!

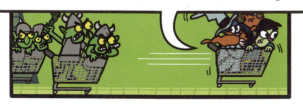

Ummm ... how do you steer this thing?

Arrrgggghhhhh!

About the author

Hello. I'm Seb. I grew up in Lincolnshire but now live in Bristol with my wife and daughter. I work as an illustrator and animator so I get to make up stories and draw monsters every day. I also like biscuits.

The Quest is a true story, actually. I live next door to Dramalina's mum and she told me all about it.